CONTEMPORARY WRITERS IN CHRISTIAN PERSPECTIVE
EDITED BY RODERICK JELLEMA

22-84

John
Updike

A CRITICAL ESSAY
BY ALICE and
KENNETH HAMILTON

WILLIAM B. EERDMANS/PUBLISHER

To

C. L. B.

a man of insight

CONTENTS

A SENSE OF PLACE

Only yesterday an upstarting, youthful prodigy, today John Updike is one of the permanent features on the scene of American fiction. Unusually productive, he has to his credit since 1958 four novels, three volumes of short stories, two volumes of poems, three books for children, and a collection of essays, parodies, and reviews. Everyone admits that he has talent to burn and an accomplished style; but, after that, the critics divide sharply. Some acclaim him a major literary figure, the brightest star in American letters since Salinger, and possibly the most creative writer to emerge since World War Two. Others complain that his accomplishment, from the first decorative rather than substantial, proves itself with each new publication to be progressively less important: more about next to nothing.

The photographs on the dust jackets of his books show us a humorous, expressive, memorable face, beak-nosed and oddly puckish in its suggestion of being at once very young and very old. There is a similar elfin trickery about his work, a smell of hidden complexities behind the apparently frank prose, that makes us wonder whether his fiction wears an air of wisdom it does not possess or whether it pretends to be much slighter than it really is. So the disagreement among the critics about his claim to be considered a "serious" writer is easy to understand. Yet, take him one way or the other, Updike remains something of a puzzle. Even his basic stance as a writer is hard to pin down. He has been called an intellectual who studies his characters from a distance and fails to become involved with them; and a back-to-nature romantic who moves entirely in the thoughtless sphere of feeling. He has been claimed as an apologist for traditional Christianity; and as a skeptical critic of conventional religion.

At any rate, he has never tried to adopt the pose of the grand artist who will not explain himself except through the pure medium of his art. He is accessible to interviewers, and speaks freely of his own opinions and beliefs, his past achievements and future plans, his views on the craft of writing, and his estimate of his contemporaries. Still, in spite of his willingness to talk, the one thing about Updike that is not open to question is his subject-matter. He has frequently asserted that his fiction is rooted in his personal memories. So it is with Updike the man that we must begin.

The outward events to date in the life of John Hoyer Updike—Hoyer is his mother's name—can soon be summarized. An only child of parents with Dutch, German, and Irish forebears, he was born in 1932 in the small town of Shillington, Pennsylvania. His father was a high-school teacher, and his mother had a life-long interest in writing. When John was thirteen, his family moved from their large Shillington home to a farmhouse in the country near Plowville, not far away. His mother's father had made money, but lost it in the Depression, so that the family was poverty-conscious. When a scholarship opened John's way to Harvard his mother was confident that he was set on his course to be a writer, though he saw himself as a cartoonist. At Harvard he drew cartoons and wrote prose and poetry for the *Lampoon,* graduating *summa cum laude* in 1954, and marrying Mary Pennington, a fine-arts major from Radcliffe. There followed a year on a fellowship at the Ruskin School of Drawing and Fine Art in Oxford, England. That year he realized his childhood ambition to be published in *The New Yorker,* and was offered a position on its staff. From 1955 to 1957 he was with *The New Yorker,* acting as reporter for "Talk of the Town." Since then he has been a full-time author. The Updikes and their four children now live at Ipswich, Massachusetts. Most of John's short stories and poems continue to make their first appearance in *The New Yorker,* and in recent years his mother also has had short stories published there.

The link between Updike's life and art is found spelled out most plainly in "The Dogwood Tree: A Boyhood," an essay written for a symposium of American childhoods, and reprinted in his 1965 volume *Assorted Prose*. In particular, it contains one revealing sentence: "My father's job paid him poorly, but me well; it gave a sense of, not prestige, but *place*." (The italics are Updike's.)

8

Our age is one that has coined an unpleasing phrase for a menacing, typically twentieth-century phenomenon: "displaced person." Updike is very well aware that the consciousness of possessing a solid sense of place is a rarity today. He notes soberly that the stability of his own childhood was purchased at the price of catastrophe in the world at large—the Depression and the Second World War. Those who would dismiss his work as uninvolved in the tragedies of our times ignore his clear sight of the context of the ordinary. Updike's universe may look enclosed and parochial, too slight and too safe to contain the tragedy and terror that occupy the headlines of our disordered days. But he holds to a faith that does not despair of finding order in chaos and a stillness at the heart of the maelstrom. On the basis of his experience of finding a place where human values may be nourished and mature, he maintains that extremes, incoherent in themselves, meet in a middle point; and that man may still rest, if he will, upon the eternal simplicities that our earth sustains. In "The Dogwood Tree" he speaks of the vision that held him as he first explored the activity of art.

> Blankness is not emptiness; we may skate upon an intense radiance we do not see because we see nothing else. And in fact there is a color, a quiet but tireless goodness that things at rest, like a brick wall or a small stone, seem to affirm. A wordless reassurance these things are pressing to give. An hallucination? To transcribe middleness with all its grits, bumps, and anonymities, in its fullness of satisfaction and mystery: is it possible, or, in view of the suffering that violently colors the periphery and that at all moments threatens to move into the center, worth doing? Possibly not; but the horse-chestnut trees, the telephone poles, the porches, the green hedges recede to a calm point that in my subjective geography is still the center of the world.

To maintain that the world has a center is heresy in the eyes of those who preach the absurdity of existence. And to locate that center in remembered things is equally abhorrent to the dogmatists insisting that contemporary man is a new species repudiating all the values of the past. Updike knows that his convictions are unpopular ones. Yet he is not afraid to be called an escapist, since what self-styled realists think to be central is for him peripheral; and what they judge to be the easy way out he knows to be the hard way in. Here he is instructed chiefly by the example of the writers of the past who, on both sides of the Atlantic, have formed the tradition of English prose, but also by his own sensibility.

In a review of Alan Sillitoe's *The Loneliness of the Long-Distance Runner* Updike advances the proposition that the writer's basic problem is to connect "the experiences, usually accumulated by the age of twenty, that seem worth telling about, and the sophistication needed to render them in writing." His method of avoiding being defeated by "simplifying distance," which he sees as the prime enemy of literary integrity, is to return continually to the place where the experiences worth telling about were first gained. Thus Shillington, under its fictional name of Olinger, is frequently revisited; and we see the Peters and Davids and Jays of the Olinger stories—Johns most thinly disguised—making their way through childhood and adolescence along familiar streets under the eyes of almost identical parents and grandparents. Autobiography would not do the trick, however, had Updike not welded from the first the external landscape to the internal one. As it is, he is able to use his sense of place to bring together space and time, actuality and imaginative reality, reason and emotion.

Spatially, Shillington was the center of a child's universe. Concentric circles billowed outward, like ripples on the water from a thrown stone, from the large white house and its adjacent streets to the edge of the town explored on Sunday walks; from there to the Pennsylvania countryside beyond, with smoke from a larger town, Reading (fictional Alton), visible on the horizon; and, beyond that, to the whole of the United States and the great, unimaginable world itself. So the environment had a definite shape and specific, though not restrictive, boundaries. In human terms, as well, space had its reasonable shape for a child who was the schoolteacher's son and saw his father involved in community affairs and in the local church. Both at work and play he moved in a known area that nevertheless did not fence him in, for the familiar landmarks could suddenly manifest contours of the mysterious and the infinite.

The shape of time was less evident, since it was through lesser or greater catastrophes shattering the normal routine of life that its presence was felt. The death of Roosevelt, for example, was followed by the family move from town-house to farm, impressing upon young John how time, like space, had its wide expanses and its boundaries. His grandparents represented

10

for him a middle ground between his parents and himself—the basic family unit—and the horizon of the past; for their lives were more or less strange to him. He knew them rather in the reflected picture he gained through his mother's attitude toward them, an attitude forged by events taking place before he was born. Thus the active continuity of the generations, where life touched life along in the chain of the years, was an immediate datum of experience. Time too had its concentric circles, its interdependent spaces. To the family it seemed, indeed, more than a coincidence that John should marry a Mary Pennington, when the Updikes had come, only two generations back, from Pennington, New Jersey.

"The Dogwood Tree" explains that the passage from childhood to adolescence brings an encounter with three "mysteries": sex, religion, and art. Updike's fiction is largely preoccupied with showing how these mysteries, woven early into the texture of our lives, color all the episodes of our mature existence. As we try to find a direction for our lives, consciously striving towards those values that seem to us to be important, our first experiences of grappling with the three imponderables always remain determinative. Even when we revolt against our past and aim to set our sights in a new direction, what we were still moulds what we are. This is not to deny the reality or the importance of the choices we make along the way; it is to assert that we are usually quite misled by the explanations we give ourselves at the time of decision. The narrator of Updike's short story "The Music School" muses, ". . . in the end each life wears its events with a geological inevitability." Like the landscape in which we move, we are the product of a long process. The layers of the self are accumulated by experience and eroded by circumstance.

So Updike's skill is employed in presenting us with a picture of separate lives set in a complex yet orderly universe where to be human is to be creatively involved with mysteries. In his estimate of the well-spent life he allows little weight to mere cleverness or strength of will; the varieties of intelligence and stupidity, on the one hand, and of boldness and timidity, on the other, occupy his attention a good deal as he makes his writer's report upon humanity. Ultimately, however, not knowledge and power but wisdom and faith are for him the harvest of the years. Faith is the positive relationship engendering stability and tranquillity: faith between persons, between man and all creation, between man and his Creator. And the preservation of faith through suffering and temptation brings the achievement of wisdom, a vision of reality bringing with it the reward of enduring joy.

Blankness, says Updike, is not emptiness. Many would deny the distinction, for this is not an age that puts its money upon faith; blankness and emptiness are often coupled together and held to characterize the modern experience. Updike gains the dramatic tensions evident throughout his work by describing how the intimations of radiance illuminating the space where we walk struggle against the seemingly plain evidence that emptiness prevails around us. Often in his writings the omnipresence of un-faith in the adult world is countered only by a cherished memory of childhood convictions affirming life and love. At other times we hear of small yet significant victories won over doubt and confusion, establishing a new balance of hope against despair; these are victories that have to be fought for all the way from early youth to full maturity.

Because a sense of place is the chief tactical advantage we can possess in the mental warfare of our existence, the loss of a sense of community in the wide spaces of city life is also a recurring theme in Updike's fiction. In spite of familiarity with its features, New York City does not receive very kindly treatment from him, and satire seems to come to the fore when he describes "the Madison Avenue men." But he has no animus against cities as such. His accusation is that *all* society is estranged from the sources that nourish its proper good.

Slight as may seem to be the equipment he possesses for the purpose of bringing to judgment a whole civilization, Updike handles it with confidence and poise. War, famine, and revolution abroad; crime, violence, race-hatred, and corruption in high places at home: those are not the coin he deals in. But in the uneasiness of a husband about the faithfulness of his wife, or in the elation of a high-school student's spirits as he walks home with his companions after a football game, he catches the quality of the air that we are all breathing today. And, a shrewd analyst, he tells us what the effects of inhaling it are likely to be and how long we are likely to survive in it.

II

HOW FARES AMERICA?

THE POORHOUSE FAIR

Updike has put on record that he does not wish his fiction to appear less ambiguous than life; and mostly he stays within his intention. A few of his stories, indeed, carry one enigmatic concluding sentence that claims to sum up what the story has been about. Only rarely does he provide his readers with anything more, or allow the imagery of his narrative to be broken by a direct "message." The exception is his first novel *The Poorhouse Fair* (1959).

The subject of the novel is taken from one of the author's childhood memories. The wall of the poorhouse in Shillington was to be seen at the end of the street where he was born. His father, almost convinced that he would end his days inside it, used to joke that it was a comfort to know that he had only a short distance to walk when his time came. Once a year the townsfolk could come inside the wall for the day of the poorhouse fair, meeting their neighbors and buying the old folk's simple handicrafts. Yet in recreating this well-remembered day, Updike puts the event deliberately in the future instead of the past. Whenever novelists project us forward in time we may be sure that they are assuming the role of social critic, telling us what to expect after good or evil tendencies in our society have had time to develop to their logical conclusion. With *The Poorhouse Fair* Updike joins the company of Huxley and Orwell in predicting the Utopia of horror, the hell we're headed for. Updike's hell is near enough the world we know now not to look particularly horrific. But the motto prefixed to the book gives a warning from the Bible (Luke 23:31): "If they do this when the wood is green, what will happen when the wood is dry?"

Having nudged the years on into the early seventies, Updike shows us an America freed from the Cold War and from internal tensions and free to plan for unlimited prosperity. For the people in New Jersey (Shillington's poorhouse has been moved slightly East), the shape of things to come is evident mainly in the increase of the power of bureaucracy. This is typified in the persons of Conner, the poorhouse "prefect," and Buddy his assistant, who is expert at typing complicated reports. Although in his three years of running the poorhouse Conner has made many overdue improvements, he has failed to win the confidence of the inmates. On the day of their annual fair they at last find an expression for their corporate disapproval of him. He asks them to carry away the debris from the poorhouse wall after a truck bringing soft drinks to the fair has knocked down a section by the gateway. They stone him on impulse, not hard enough to break bones but sufficiently hard to convince him of their acute antagonism, which he interprets as moronic ingratitude. Yet the fair, earlier expected to be cancelled because of rain, goes on; and the day ends with the annual ritual taking its customary course in spite of the passing threats of weather and imposed authority.

Among the crowd of three-dimensional characters created by Updike in this book, Conner emerges as an oddly two-dimensional figure. This is not just because he represents a type, for nearly all the author's characters have typical significance. Rather, it seems that Updike regards him with such distaste that he makes him merely typical, an object-lesson instead of a human being. We can almost hear Updike murmuring to us that this sort of individual is less than human, and thus *cannot* come off the printed page as a real person. Conner certainly is drawn without one creditable feature or amiable eccentricity. He is even denied pre-eminence in his faults; and walks the way to hell paved with good intentions. He is a humanist without knowledge of humanity except as a sentimental ideal, an altruist whose visions of serving mankind dissolve into pictures of himself being congratulated in committee rooms, and a believer in progress with his eyes fixed upon advancement in the bureaucratic hierarchy. Uncomprehending before the mystery and awesomeness of the universe, he "cons" the external face of nature with the conviction that it can be moulded to fit his insipid dreams. He cannot conceive that the way things are is

14

more important than the way he sees them, or that there is more in heaven and earth than his philosophy allows. Consequently it seems to him that he is always being thwarted by "unfortunate" circumstances and "unreliable" people. His ignorance of nature and of man is compounded in his utter lack of self-knowledge. Self-convinced of his good-will toward the old folk in his charge and the injustice of their hostility toward him, he looks down from his office window and says, "Damn these people."

His malediction falls principally upon John F. Hook, ex-school teacher and, at ninety-four, the oldest inmate. Basically, Conner's dislike of Hook is born of mediocrity's desire to destroy excellence. Hook, for his part, sees Conner as weak and "sorely striken." While his companions rage against the latest affront to their dignity imposed by the official mind, Hook tries to restrain them by explaining, "A child like Conner must tinker endless-ly." Yet Conner is sure that Hook is continually plotting against him. Because Hook happens to be nearby when the stoning begins, he sees this as clear proof that it is a planned operation—so carefully planned, indeed, that he has failed to notice the old man giving the signal for battle. Having explained to the stone-throwers that they are forgiven, he vindictively deprives Hook of his cigar on the pretext that it is a danger to health and safety. Earlier in the day, too, this enemy has withstood his cogent argument that belief in God is an absurdity, turning aside each thrust and ending with the comment: "There is no goodness, without belief. There is nothing but busy-ness." Who could forgive that?

It has been objected that a poorhouse is an inept symbol of the welfare state, since the very word has been dropped by social workers. The point is that the fact of the poorhouse being needed refutes the progressivist philosophy, as Hook refutes Conner's skepticism. While their prefect rhapsodizes over the elimination of poverty, the inmates realistically remind him how the process has already overfilled their building. The aged are unwanted in homes where the little money they can offer is no longer a consideration. Updike's scorn is poured upon a generation who find it shameful, not to do evil, but to name it; who forbid the word "poorhouse," but multiply the number who live as paupers. He emphasizes that Conner is the disciple of those who are prepared, not wholly as a joke, to advocate mass murder. But he presents the physically feeble, who are so easily judged superfluous to society, as the source of society's spiritual power. Conner cannot guess what draws the townspeople to the fair, and Buddy tells him that they just come to see a freak show. A very different explanation is given by Updike's description of the arrival of the visitors.

> Heart had gone out of these people; health was the principal thing about the faces of the Americans that came crowding through the broken wall to the poorhouse fair. They were just people, members of the race of white animals that had cast its herds over the land of six continents. . . . History had passed on beyond them. They remembered its moment and came to the fair to be freshened in the recollection of an older America, the America of Dan Patch and of Senator Beveridge exhorting the Anglo-Saxons to march across the Pacific and save the beautiful weak-minded islands there, an America of stained-glass lampshades, hardshell evangelists, Flag Days, ice men, plug tobacco, China trade, oval windows marking on the exterior of a house a stair landing within, pungent nostrums for catarrhal complaints, opportunism, churchgoing, and well-worded orations in the glare of a cemetery on summer days.

Mere nostalgia for the not-so-good old days? Updike recognizes that some fair-goers were attracted chiefly by the superficial aspects of bygone America around them: the patchwork quilts and the salty talk of the old-timers. Nevertheless, whether they knew it or not they received a much more basic refreshment of the heart, because they had come out of the sphere of the merely contemporary—life in the meaningless flux of passing moments—into the sphere of history, where events are stamped with purpose and are integrated into significant patterns.

Conner has no use for patterns; he strives to impose simple, rigid plans upon the unpredictable variety of nature. His vision is "of Man living healthy and unafraid beneath blank skies." For him, blankness *is* emptiness. So he is annoyed when Hook's forecast of the weather proves more accurate than that of the official forecasters. Hook, the teacher whose work it has been to pass the living wisdom of civilization from one generation to another, does not think of Man in the abstract. He sees each face he meets in the present in terms of the students he recalls, by name, from his past. Instead of blank skies, his vision is linked to the years when he lived beside the Delaware and watched the changing colors of that historic water.

Hook is the perfect foil to Conner in that he respects reality. Instead of trying to impose arid theory upon the universe, he patiently reads the face of nature and of man. The pattern of life, he has learned, takes time to decipher. So he is a student of history—a specialist in Roman history and in nineteenth-century American politics. His long life, so Updike tells us, has been like a walk down a gallery hung with portraits of American presidents. Updike's own report on the present state of America, "The nation became one of pleasure-seekers; the people continued to live as cells of a body do in a coffin, for the conception 'America' has died in their skulls," is followed immediately by Hook's comment that Nero's age was likewise one of pleasure, peace, and perversion. Hook, here and elsewhere, links Nero with Lincoln. He refuses to accept the popular opinion of Lincoln as an idealist and a humanitarian, insisting that he was in private life an atheist, and in public life a front for the corrupt interests that showed themselves in the administration of "Lincoln's man Grant." Updike seems to have set his novel deliberately a century after the time of the scandals arising during Grant's presidency.

Critics have complained that in *The Poorhouse Fair* much is made of small happenings. The strength of the book is that, as in the fiction of Jane Austen or Henry James or James Joyce, small happenings serve large purposes because they lead us into the heart of a complex pattern. The obvious opposition between Conner and Hook as exponents of contrasting creeds lets us see that Updike's theme in this novel is a struggle for the soul of America. But the struggle is worked out concretely in terms of how the true American survives in the poorhouse, and is exhibited on the day when its life is "on show" to the outside world.

Conner argues with Hook, but the poorhouse building itself silently protests against his ideals. Built by Walter Andrews at the turn of the century, its well-carpentered structure proclaims a personal purpose at odds with the impersonal efficiency worshipped by its present prefect. (We should pause to notice that fine carpentry has a special meaning for Updike. It is significant that his first published book had the title *The Carpentered Hen*. In the short story "The Archangel" the celestial Being of the title promises a dwelling built with just those details of precise joints that Hook recalls as characteristic of the master workmen of his youth. Hook remarks that the profession of carpenter was the one most fitting for God made flesh to assume. Thus Updike makes clear that both Christ and His representatives

17

have identified themselves with craftsmanship in a living material.) Crowning the Andrews house is a cupola, once the music-room and now the prefect's office. The room was originally built round the large piano which, since it cannot be moved, remains hemmed in by steel cabinets. Conner hates the symbolic height of the cupola, and comes down to eat and talk with his charges. But the old folk think he is only making himself look common. His predecessor, Mendelssohn, ate raised on a dais; and he used to lead them in community singing, ending with hymns, prayers, and homilies on the omnipresence of death. They understood the nineteenth-century romantic "music" of this latter-day Mendelssohn, who looked so pious and dignified in life, and in his coffin, although he spent his days drinking and neglected the care of the place. He knew what he was doing when he chose the lofty music-room for his sanctum. Conner, though "like many humanists . . . deeply responsive to music," is out of tune with the old people's tastes. He cannot "perform" to please them.

The ball-room wing of the house has been turned into the hospital. Conner takes special pride in his improvements here. But what human comfort there is in the space now turned over to the dance of death is provided by the presence of the nurse Grace. Against the rules Grace brings in some young friends during the fair in order to show her "poor sicklies" they are not forgotten. In spite of the clumsiness of the visitors' efforts to give physical comfort to the patients, this act of "grace" evokes their gratitude. It will not find a place in Conner's statistics; yet its grace note registers.

Even the poorhouse wall has a voice to accuse Conner. Built by Andrews to say "Mine" rather than "Keep Away," it crumbles easily when hit by the soft-drinks truck. Unlike the house itself it is not well built. Personal possession is an impermanent thing. Conner feels that the fallen rubble is a public confession that he cannot keep the poorhouse in good order, and his attempt to clear it up leads to the debacle of the stoning. But, symbolically more important, at the moment when the wall is struck, he does not see what has happened. The sound strikes his ears as thunder out of a clear sky. This was the phenomenon, so Updike tells us, that once was taken by Horace to prove the existence of the gods. Today the very man who undertakes to prove the non-existence of deity is thus informed of the Wrath of Heaven against impiety.

The new prefect, unable to comprehend that the past is in living continuity with the present, misses the lesson taught by the Andrews building. He is unaware that his hurt surprise over the weakness of the wall betrays the shallowness of his illusion that old age and illness can be kept away from society. He does not know the wall never said "Keep Away." Equally, he pays little attention to the views of the inmates of the poorhouse who cannot articulate their ideas.

After Hook, with whom she is not afraid to argue, the most vocal of the old folk is Amy Mortis. She tells Conner that he is wrong to imagine that he can fashion their lives after the ways of the modern world; and, upon his admission that his vision of a heaven-upon-earth will not come in their day, she responds with a forthright, "Well, then, to hell with it." Her name, like that of Grace and Mendelssohn, displays her function. A Friend of Death, she sees no value in prolonging life, "when if we had any sense we'd let the Lord take us and start off fresh." In Hook's age group, she yearly makes patchwork quilts to sell at the fair. There will be no more, she insists, after this fair. Not only is she too old, but also she finds it increasingly difficult to obtain patterned material. These days, the blank skies favored by Conner are reflected in the cloth that women demand. Once again Updike gives symbolic suggestiveness to commonplace detail. Here and elsewhere intricate pattern suggests the glory of both nature and human existence. The one shows the power of the Creator, and the other the joy of the craftsman (e.g., carpenter or musician) in creative work. Two of Updike's books are named after stories concerned with the two kinds of pattern: *Pigeon Feathers* and *The Music School.*

Hook is called by Updike "the man of thought." Two younger inmates, Lucas and Gregg, are identified respectively as "the man of flesh" and "the man of passion." Lucas, a family man, shares his room with his weak-legged wife Martha and a green parakeet wished on them by their daughter Joan. He irritates his sore ear with a match, and irritates Conner also by intruding upon him with complaints. He is the symbol of the nagging weakness of the body. When the parakeet escapes from their room, Lucas follows its random flight and finally catches it in the room of a dying man. Flesh, a flying green bird, is doomed to capture in the end. And those who live only in the flesh do not value human life. Joan had given her parents the bird simply because it was a nuisance, and she herself, a bird in flight, had no settled home. Lucas gains a little pleasure from his job of feeding the poorhouse pigs, nourishing beasts reared to be killed. Flesh feeds on flesh.

Gregg, unmarried, foul-mouthed, ill-tempered and physically timid, rages with tireless energy against Conner—behind his back. An illiterate romantic poet, his outlook is so incomprehensible to Conner that his presence never registers with him. Yet it is Gregg who succeeds in wounding him, twice over. For Gregg is the one who first has the impulse to aim a stone at Conner when the inmates are called to tidy up the broken wall. The knowledge that he has at last translated his dreams into action causes Gregg to dance with joy when he is alone after the others have gone to bed at the end of the fair. But, unknown to him, he has caused Conner a deeper wound than the stones inflicted. The prefect cannot put out of his mind the phrases of an anonymous letter he has received, signed "A 'Town's person.'" From his trust in textbooks on psychology he cherishes the conviction that a warped spinster has written it. His naïveté (which seems to be shared by at least one critic) springs from his knowing nothing of Gregg's language or imagination. As in the event of the stoning, he blames the wrong person because he has no notion of the power of feeling, of the feminine in the masculine. For all Gregg's surface unpleasantness, Hook understands his charm. This misfit has a child's amoral yet direct perception that short-cuts the processes of reasoning and finds the intuitive route to truth. It is Gregg who reacts violently to Conner's tagging the inmates' chairs with their names, ostensibly to foster a pride of ownership. Gregg sees it as the wish to treat them like pigs, docketed by their owner. (He despises Lucas, the pig-feeder.) And it is Gregg who carries inside the wall a cat injured by being run over by a car, and rages when Buddy shoots it on Conner's orders. Hook points out that it was better out of its misery, but Gregg understands that the death of the cat represents officialdom's power of life and death over them all, wounded as they are by the wheels of progress. He is right, for Conner thinks when he hears the shot that it is the sound of space being made for the brave new world that will arrive once all his old people are gone.

The words in Gregg's letter that the prefect cannot put out of his mind are these: "Yr duty is to help not hinder these old people on the way to their final Reward." The letter as such frightens Conner, because criticism from outside the poorhouse wall endangers his career. This particular sentence, though, touches him at a deeper level. Consciously, he finds its sentiment repellent. What reward can the aged have except the one he is devoting his time to give them, a well-run institution in which to spend their last years? Unconsciously, he knows that he would like to hurry them on their way to the reward meted out to the dying cat. He cannot bear to face directly the contradictions latent in his humanitarian creed which, by making healthy physical existence the one good, obliterates the human image and turns men into brutes. Gregg is not able to reason with Conner in Hook's terms. Yet his misspelled words in their anger deliver their message more effectively than does Hook's highly literate warning: "And if you have not believed, at the end of your life you should know you have buried your talent in the ground of this world and have nothing saved, to take into the next."

Updike knows that every artist uses Gregg's voice rather than Hook's. So in *The Poorhouse Fair* he opposes to the wished-for blank skies of the community planners the visible cloud-filled skies, alternating between storm and fitful sunshine, above the poorhouse on its fair-day. Like Amy Mortis sewing her patchwork quilts out of scraps combined to form an intricate pattern, he makes much of little things. Hook is not only a teacher and a man of faith; he is also a symbolic near-century of American history, having eyes that pierce the distance and see with difficulty what is near at hand. He is a hook drawing the past into relation with the present (maybe Updike has in mind that old-fashioned, reliable fastener, the "hook and eye"!). When he examines Amy Mortis's latest quilt he finds there a piece of material having the pattern of his boyhood bedspread. Pattern is what Updike gives us—a hundred years of America in stone and wood, sky and grass, argument and reverie, laughter and curses. Toward the end of the book, quilt-like patches of conversation across the generations are stitched together without comment. And we see the young, in fear and fascination, eyeing the mystery of naked female flesh in the headlights of their cars at the time when the old, tired and forgetful, prepare their bodies for sleep.

Almost, the new masters of the world have had their desire. Almost, the ways of tradition have been broken. For one more year, with the coming of "fair" weather, the healing ritual has been enacted. But the evening skies were stormy, and the future is uncertain. Next year—through the next century—how will America fare?

III

LONG THOUGHTS IN SHORT STORIES

THE SAME DOOR AND *PIGEON FEATHERS*

The Same Door contains short stories written between 1954 and 1958. This book, Updike's first collection of his *New Yorker* stories, came out in the year of his first novel. A second collection, *Pigeon Feathers*, appeared in 1962, and a third, *The Music School*, in 1966.

What Updike has to say he says first in his short stories. His novels are, in a sense, second tries.

Ordinarily, there is very little plot in an Updike short story. We are given what seem to be casual impressions—candid camera shots recording a mass of detail that just happens to obtrude in front of the lens. Updike appears as meticulous in observation as a camera, and apparently almost as unselective. Well, the detail is there all right, yet in fact the selection is as rigorous as the observation is precise. If we take the stories together rather than separately, we can be in no doubt that they focus upon a limited number of related themes. Through imagery and symbolism each tale makes a small but forceful point, that builds up, with cumulative effect, into an extended statement. This author is no slick reporter. He is a commentator with a reflecting mind that modifies his perceptions.

That the stories are more than disconnected impressions is indicated by the fact that at least two sets of characters recur

22

several times in the collections. These are two married couples: Richard and Joan Maple, and Jack and Clare. The latter, like many of Updike's characters, are given no surname. It may seem odd that both the Maples and Jack and Clare mention having spent the first three months of their marriage in a Y.M.C.A. Holiday Camp, but then the tendency of all the characters is to share a common background of experience similar to that of the Updikes. The events in their lives are also likely to coincide chronologically with events in the Updike family life, and to happen in identical or comparable places.

The Same Door exhibits some symmetry in the location of its stories. Three stories set in Pennsylvania open the collection, followed by a single one set in Oxford and nine about young couples who have come to live in New York City. Then another singleton set in Connecticut precedes two final "Olinger" Pennsylvania tales. The stories forming the frame of the book give point to the two quotations supplied at the beginning: in one Bergson is speaking of how our pleasures are mainly furnished by memory, and in the other Eliot is celebrating the luminosity of family love. It is entirely conceivable, indeed, that to these two quotations might have been added a third, namely,

> My heart leaps up when I behold
> A rainbow in the sky:
> So was it when my life began;
> So is it now I am a man;
> So be it when I shall grow old,
> Or let me die!
> The Child is father of the Man;
> And I could wish my days to be
> Bound each to each by natural piety.

Of course, Wordsworth's familiar poem applies no more to this book of Updike's than to the rest. But it does apply quite conspicuously. *The Same Door* is a record of days either bound joyously by natural piety or disappointingly fragmented because they are not so bound.

Predictably, the stories set in New York City are nearly all about disappointment. Moving to the metropolis means a rupture in our sense of place that cannot but disorganize our days. In "Incest" Updike shows us a couple whose efforts to keep the healthy continuity of life intact under the pressures of their environment produce odd results. They are both trying, unsuccessfully, to get through the volumes of Proust's *Remembrance*

23

of Things Past when the husband Lee begins to identify, in dreams and waking thought, his wife, his mother-in-law, and his baby girl. City life usually destroys the links between the generations, yet in this case the links have been drawn unnaturally tight. The sense of the unnatural is conveyed by Lee's referring to the Proust volume he is currently reading as "Sodom and Gemorrah." He translates the French title into the language of his own situation, avoiding the less explicit English title *Cities of the Plain*. Lee is the more easily drawn into imaginative "incest" because his wife and daughter are both called Jane.

Perhaps the book's most emphatic portrayal of the opposition between the spontaneous vision maintained in a complete life and the broken existence of the city dweller is found in "Toward Evening." Rafe comes home from work on the bus, bringing with him a box containing a mobile for his baby girl. (Baby girls are much in evidence at the time when Updike had one daughter.) The mobile features seven birds with celluloid wings. Rafe's wife Alice is disappointed that it is not a Calder mobile with polished wooden birds; his daughter just wants to stuff it in her mouth. After dinner Rafe sits looking out over the Hudson where a flashing neon sign dominates the sky.

Help in interpreting Updike's thinking here is forthcoming from one of his "Talk of the Town" pieces reprinted in *Assorted Prose* and from a *New Yorker* poem "Mobile of Birds" (1959) reprinted in *Telephone Poles* (1964). In the former we read,

> No matter how long we live among rectangular stones, we still listen, in the pauses of a rain, for the sound of birds chirping as they shake themselves.

And the latter begins,

> There is something
> In their planetary weaving that is comforting.

The poem goes on to say that the motion is "random as nature" yet "calculable," recalling "those old Ptolemaic heavens."

So birds represent, in the first place, natural life stirring in the dead forms of the city. On the bus Rafe notices three female passengers: an old woman, a young woman, and a negress. Each in turn suggests to him the form of a different bird. In the second place, birds on a mobile suggest a coherent universe.

There are seven birds (the perfect number) on Rafe's mobile. But their wings are celluloid, and so linked with a cellulose sign Rafe sees on the bus. This is an "ingenious" affair advertising coffee. It is meant to show a coffee drinker in two positions; however, from the angle of Rafe's seat both images appear simultaneously, and this spoils the illusion. Similarly, the flashing sign on the rooftops gives alternating messages, "Spry FOR BAKING: Spry FOR FRYING." This sign blots out the stars. The mechanical, man-made motions of the city are jerky, broken, blurred.

From the bus, too, Rafe sees the numbers of the houses, connecting each with a date in history. The first he notes is 1850, the year of Wordsworth's death. Other dates are: 1914 . . . Joyce begins *Ulysses* and war begins in Europe; 1926 . . . Rafe's parents marry in Ithica; 1936 . . . Rafe is four years old (Updike also).

> Where the present should have stood, a block was torn down, and the numbering began again with 2000, a boring progressive edifice.

It would seem that "Toward Evening" indicates the eclipse of history, the destruction of human values in the present, and the coming of a new Dark Age when the heavens hold no comforting vision and man is broken by his mechanical ingenuity.

There is another theme, though, important if less obvious. "Toward Evening" recalls the biblical story of the walk to Emmaus. "Abide with us: for it is toward evening, and the day is far spent," say the disciples (Luke 24:29), and the Risen Lord breaks bread with them. Nature sees to it that we must, in any age, eat and drink. Even cellulose signs advertise coffee. Rafe's daughter naturally stuffs the birds in her mouth. Rafe's dinner is a near-sacrament, for it is made up of his favorite foods, the gifts of his wife's care for him. And, at the table, a piece of bread drops from her hand "like a star." Although Spry signs obscure the visible heavens, heaven endures while family love is known. The day of coherent human purpose in harmony with cosmic wholeness is far spent. But the night of progressive boredom has not descended. It is a threat in the future. Before the year 2000 arrives the gap in history may have been filled.

In these two examples of Updike's art we see three elements that are explored ever more searchingly as his writing progresses.

First, the natural human unit is the family. In describing loneliness Updike makes a clear distinction between the inevitable separateness of each individual who must live his own life and make his own decisions and the unnatural, atomistic separateness of modern life. The Child is indeed father of the Man, and in their early experience of the family children have their chance to discover how interdependence on the basis of trust constitutes the truly human dimension of life. A loving home lays the foundation for that sense of place, allowing the individual to relate himself to friends, to neighbors, to fellow citizens, and to the universe itself.

Second, sexuality makes the family possible. Every child is the fruit of the union of one man with one woman, and the quality of his environment depends upon how his parents handle their masculinity and femininity. Updike's women are sometimes more sophisticated than their menfolk, but their strength lies in their intuitive grasp of reality and in their keeping near to nature. So in "Incest" Lee's wife instinctively protests Lee's decision to name their daughter Jane, although the reason she gives—she does not want to be called "big Jane"—looks trivial. And Rafe's wife Alice, though fond of ultra-modern plates, serves on them simple meals that feed her husband's soul.

Third, the pattern of complementary differences that marks the family (masculinity and femininity, maturity and dependence, sexual passion and social affection) relates us to the total pattern of the universe. That is why the idea of progress is "boring." It suggests that we are free to scrap the past and build according to our fancy. But, once we have broken with the past, we have destroyed the texture of nature's balanced pattern. We have nowhere to go except into blankness. We have skies without stars or birds, while on the earth the generations become confused and man is reduced to a blurred image, immobilized and fearfully alone.

The final pair of stories in *The Same Door* return from unnatural to natural existence. In "Alligators" Updike shows how, in Olinger, the apparent cruelty of grade five children to a stranger from Maryland is genuine love. The pattern of personal relationships may be ambiguous, but it is creative and forces all who participate in it to grow in wisdom. "The Happiest I've Been" is a picture of a moment when, poised between adolescence and maturity, one life realizes its unity with the larger pattern of existence. On his way to see the girl who is to become his wife, the narrator drives his friend's car with his friend sleeping beside him. He feels pride in Pennsylvania—his state —pride that his friend trusts him, and pride that his life, like the countryside, lies before him to journey through. "I had seen a dawn," he says. It is the exact inverse of the situation in "Toward Evening." *There* unnatural darkness threatened. *Here* man's heart leaps up as the sky brightens into morning, and his joy merges into nature's glory.

With *Pigeon Feathers and Other Stories* Updike strikes more deeply, and with surer touch, into the heart of life's patterns. The motto affixed to the collection is Kafka's confession of how, as he becomes progressively more at home among men, the aperture of memory shrinks. There is less superficial cleverness in the later book than in *The Same Door,* less satire, and less gaiety. Updike seems sobered by the thought that it is not enough to know that we ought to return to the same door we knew in childhood. The door may have closed against us. So he probes man's effort to understand not merely the natural, but the supernatural. In nearly every story the mysteries of existence—sex, religion, and art—are shown to be inseparable.

"The Astronomer" is typical of this new concern. "I feared his visit," is the opening sentence of this story of fear and faith. The astronomer is a Hungarian professor at Columbia, a bachelor and an atheist, who visits two former college friends, Walter and his wife Harriet. Walter fears Bela's intellectual weight, which, like the density of the dwarf star he once described, pulls light toward the red end of the spectrum. As Bela, charming Harriet into his orbit, leaves Walter isolated, so he strips him also of his weak religious faith. But Walter discovers, as Bela describes his vacation in the lonely black hills of New Mexico, that the astronomer has been frightened. The wise of this world, evidently, do not know all the answers posed by the stars. We must trust the moments of human, or more than human, insight that lighten our darkness.

In "The Astronomer" atheism, represented by Bertrand Russell, is balanced against faith, championed by T. S. Eliot and Søren Kierkegaard. In the title-story "Pigeon Feathers," atheism, in the form of H. G. Wells' account of the life of Jesus, meets the childish faith of thirteen-year-old David and overwhelms it. David becomes desperately concerned about his survival after death. When the Lutheran minister tells him that immortality means that Lincoln's goodness lives on after him and his mother communicates her belief that God is the product of man's creative imagination, David is in despair. Only a God that raised Jesus from the dead, and will raise him too, carries any meaning for him. Then, when he has reluctantly shot some pigeons in the barn at his grandmother's request, he looks at their plumage. The intricate patterns he sees reassure him that the God who lavished such care on expendable birds will not let David cease to be.

David's pilgrimage of faith is continued in the last story in the book "Packed Dirt, Churchgoing, A Dying Cat, A Traded Car." Here David (his full name is David Kern), married and with four children, loses faith, apparently as subjectively as he has gained it. Feeling a casual emotion of lust for a woman he has met at a party, he remembers the words of Jesus and feels that a God who thus permits him to sin in his heart does not deserve to exist. Called back to an Alton hospital where his father is dying, he is told by his mother that his father's life-long Lutheran convictions have recently vanished too.

Some critics, snatching at the all-too-obvious, have concluded that Updike regards Christianity as impossible for the mature twentieth-century man. Had Updike wished to communicate such a ridiculous commonplace in so laborious a fashion *he* would hardly deserve to exist as a writer. We know from his direct statements that the theology he has most admired is that of Karl Barth, the opponent of all demythologizing versions of Christianity; the apologetical approach of Paul Tillich, who wishes to make the Gospel intellectually acceptable to modern man, has little appeal for him. The David stories admirably illustrate the emphasis of Kierkegaard, another of Updike's teachers and the early guide of Barth; faith is the living fruit of the Moment of insight that dies unless continually renewed by the dedication of the whole man. Because the mind cannot comprehend faith, Kierkegaard insists, intellectual maturity is irrelevant to belief. Purity of heart, that wills one thing, is wholly decisive.

Like "The Astronomer," although in a more exposed form, the two David stories are studies of the pressures exerted against religious faith by our secular society. If these pressures coincide with an inner emptiness in the believer, faith collapses —momentarily, at least. Yet faithless existence is so *fear*ful a state that it cannot be permanently accepted. Faith is never disproved by skeptical arguments. Loss of faith is lack of nerve and acceptance of a servile state in which we abdicate from our humanity. To live as a human being is to cherish and practice natural piety. And, in the end, natural piety can be sustained only by belief that the joyous patterns of creation are the will of a Creator whose providential care enfolds both the external and the internal world.

Another story in *Pigeon Feathers* takes a hard look at the modern crowds who live without belief in the supernatural. "Lifeguard" tells of a theological student who spends his summers as lifeguard on a holiday beach. The student finds it hard to believe that the massed bathers, because they are a mere mass differentiated only slightly by age and sex, can be candidates for immortality. They sunbathe and swim in the shallows of the water, and never need his services in either of his professional rôles. If only once there came a cry for help, then salvation would be at hand! Even natural fear, it seems, can be ignored by those who never, to use Kierkegaard's phrase, venture far out over 50,000 fathoms of water. The Davids of this age, however, are not so insulated against reality; and they are still among us. Updike uses the second of his David stories to explain that those conscious of the contemporary disease are also partly aware of the appropriate cure.

In this story David tells how he picks up a sailor when he drives home from the hospital. The sailor is a healthy, unthinking representative of Western civilization. He is puzzled briefly over David's profession of writer. How can one spend a life writing and not be able to explain simply what one writes about? Arriving at his destination, the sailor joins his friends, evidently relieved to be back among "normal" people.

David concludes, "We in America need ceremonies, is I suppose, sailor, the point of what I have written." His record is of apparently disjointed experiences: children making paths where bulldozers have been; his pleasure in sitting beside his father in church and taking the collection; his finding a dying cat (echo of *The Poorhouse Fair*) and placing it under a hedge, with a note for its owner, at the time when his wife is in the hospital with her first baby; and his joy in driving his old car, soon to be traded, while his dying father worries about his mother not being able to take proper care of *his* old car. He finds in each incident a need for ceremony. Life, even without religious faith, demands ritual acts to give meaning to its moments.

So we return to natural piety and to Wordsworth. Man in his human dimension must have something to bind one day to the next. *At the very least* he needs to express natural piety, and that means ceremony. It is because our existence today is so fragmented that we feel alienated from nature, from one another, and from God. The symbol of modern America is the automobile that is soon discarded and scrapped without thought or concern. Our roads span the continent; yet, unlike the casual paths children make, they are not felt as happy extensions of ourselves. "We have explored, on behalf of all mankind, this paradox: the more matter is outwardly mastered, the more it overwhelms us in our hearts." Once neighborly intimacy in the small community is left behind, the ceremony of the church service becomes a forgotten language. The recognition of the need for ceremony, nevertheless, is the recognition of our continued humanity. Even a cat should not be left by a human being to die disregarded, or human birth has no significance.

In *Pigeon Feathers* Updike has gone far in developing the theme first enunciated in *The Poorhouse Fair*. There the fair that gave heart to America's dying self-awareness was seen to be important because it was traditional, a ritual. Now the rebirth of David's lost faith is prefigured in his wish to tell the sailor why he is a writer, a man commenting on the human condition as he sees it, and, at the same time, seeking for the significance of earth—and of heaven.

IV

THE HUMAN RACE

RABBIT, RUN AND *THE CENTAUR*

"Ace in the Hole" (1955), the second story in *The Same Door*, tells how Fred ("Ace") Anderson, who a few years before had been a champion basketball player at Olinger High School, is dismissed from his job at a secondhand car lot. It is not the first job he has lost, and Ace fears to break the news to his wife Evey. On his way home he stops to pick up his daughter Bonnie from his parents' house, where she has been left for the day. His mother blurts out that, if Evey walks out on them, Bonnie and he can come to live with her. Evey turns out to be as angry as Ace had expected, so in order to break the mood he turns up the radio and makes her dance with him. She rejects coldly his suggestion that their next child must be a boy who can become another champion. Yet, as she begins to pick up his rhythm in the dance, "he seemed to be great again, and all the other kids were around them, in a ring, clapping time."

This simple story, enriched and enlarged, becomes *Rabbit, Run* (1960). The basketball champion is renamed Harry ("Rabbit") Angstrom, his family is changed somewhat, and he experiences many more fluctuations of mood and fortune; yet neither he nor his fundamental problems are presented very differently in the longer work. In particular, Ace's ability to gain quiet self-confidence because he feels "so sure inside" is Rabbit's chief characteristic too. And Ace's solution for his perplexities and his difficulties with womankind is accented by Updike's transforming him into a rabbit who runs. For Ace-Rabbit, physical movement is the answer to internal doubts. What works in the game of basketball must surely work in the greater game of life.

Updike sharpens skillfully many of the details introduced into the original story. Ace has a job he dislikes and a wife who does not cook. Rabbit has a job that is patently degrading and a wife who is both slovenly and of low intelligence, forever watching TV instead of minding the home. Janice Angstrom née Springer, moreover, comes from a wealthier family than Rabbit's. Her father owns four used-car lots, and her mother considers that Janice has married beneath her. Nor can he hope, like Ace, for a son to repeat his early success. He has a son Nelson, who, as his own mother reminds him without scruple, will never make a player since he has the Springer small hands. So the ignominy of his position presses in upon him from every side. Soon it is he, not Janice, who abandons his family. When the Springers call in the Episcopal minister Eccles, whose church they belong to, Rabbit tells him that he is not going back to his home. He says he does not know how his wife feels about it. "All I know is what's inside *me*. That's all I have. Do you know what I was doing to support that bunch? I was demonstrating a penny's worth of tin called a frigging MagiPeeler in five-and-dime stores!"

From this point the plot of *Rabbit, Run* passes beyond "Ace in the Hole," for Updike presses on to show, not Ace's temporary hopes, but the permanent consequences in life of the kind of vision he cultivates. Rabbit finds consolation in Ruth, a prostitute he meets through his old coach Tothero. Ruth has a naturally affectionate nature and an earthy warmth completely lacking in Janice. But, when Janice gives birth to their baby girl June, Rabbit returns full of good intentions. Then, after this reconciliation proves unstable, Janice gets drunk and drowns June accidentally while bathing her. At the funeral Rabbit appalls Janice and both their families by blurting out that she, not he, killed the baby. Running away, he seeks Ruth again. He finds Ruth pregnant and hostile. So he runs, first to clear his head, next in "a kind of sweet panic, . . . he runs. Ah: runs. Runs." And the book ends.

If the central theme of *Rabbit, Run* is introduced in "Ace in the Hole," the complex development of the novel is something else again. The motto Updike chooses for the work is Pascal's Pensée 507: "The motions of Grace, the hardness of the heart; external circumstances." External circumstances, binding Rabbit (so he feels) like a net, are clear from the plot. The motions of grace over against the hardness of the heart are more obscure. Nevertheless, divine grace moves behind the scenes

32

throughout. As in "Toward Evening" the sacramental universe declares itself in the natural appetite for food, so here the natural sexual appetite leads to awareness of the possibility of reconciliation with God.

Sexuality is very much in evidence in the book. In this respect also the name Rabbit is brilliantly apt. But Updike's detailed descriptions of sexual intercourse, unlike so many similar passages in current writing, are not included for their own sake; they are there to make possible the use of symbolism having a far wider outreach. The key symbol in *Rabbit, Run* is found already in "Ace in the Hole." In this story the word "hole" occurs when Ace is describing how he lost his job by damaging one of the cars when he was told to park another car in a space too small to take it. "*Nobody* could have gotten into that hole," he tells his wife, "even if it had hair on it." This explicit sexual symbol explains the pun intended in the story title. Ace, in a hole of unfortunate circumstances, escapes into a creative sexual relationship with his wife. This time, he avoids the frustrations of failure through clumsiness. There can be no doubt that such is the meaning intended by his success in getting Evey to dance with him, for Updike has said that the dance is simply a socially acceptable form of sexual intercourse.

Ace connects procreation with the "kids" clapping at a basketball game. *Rabbit, Run* pinpoints this connection through Rabbit's memories of how sexual experience came in the context of excitement among the high-school population over the basketball matches. The game itself took on sexual significance in consequence. The ball had to be thrown into the hole with its "pretty skirt of net." Now that Rabbit is too old for basketball triumphs, successful sexuality is his sole link with those times when he felt "much bigger." While Rabbit's natural asset in the game had been his speed, he had also learned deftness in handling the ball; and he was a scrupulously fair player, detesting dirty or revengeful play. Tothero had taught him that to achieve is better than to win. In adult life he cannot reconcile himself to the deceits assumed to be a normal part of getting on in society. Nor can he understand vindictiveness in personal relationships; he wishes to tell the truth at whatever cost. It is this innocent belief in the virtue of not concealing one's feelings that gets him into trouble—for instance, at June's funeral.

Because of this double honesty, desiring life to be splendid, not soiled, and communication to be candid, not malicious, Rabbit has exceptional qualities. Thus some critics want to make him a quixotic saint in a nasty world. Yet Updike underlines heavily the defects of his qualities. An idealist, Rabbit is self-centered. He doesn't think much, Updike tells us, about what he gives other people. Like that other, less sensitive idealist Conner of *The Poorhouse Fair*, he prefers blank skies. Unable to appreciate the complex pattern of life that binds us to nature and to one another, he wants the "hole" without the "net" that goes with it. That is why, when the sum of things overwhelms him, he runs blindly to escape.

Ruth appeals to him as an ideal of natural sexuality. Once he has washed the heavy make-up from her face she is no longer soiled by the values of a corrupt and corrupting society. At their first meeting he asks her what she does, and she replies, "Nothing." Her eyes are the clear blue of empty skies, and it is that "nothing" that he desires. So he is appalled when he sees her eyes grow dark and stormy, and she asks for more than physical love. He has boasted that, if you have the courage to be yourself, other people will pay your price. She soon challenges his fundamental selfishness. While Rabbit continues to avoid entanglement in the net of relationships, trying to court blankness, he will gain only despair. From the first Ruth's intuition understands what he is: "Well, you're a big bunny." At the end, carrying his baby, she affirms, "You're Mr. Death himself." Subjective feeling must issue in respect for the objective world and its net of patterns. "Who cares *what* you feel?" Ruth cries.

Living realistically on the plane of nature, Ruth is impatient with Rabbit's belief in the existence of God. From her experience of men she concludes that otherworldly piety is a hypocritical cloak for animal passions. But Rabbit's belief in God is a genuine conviction that the "floor" of earth must have a "ceiling" in a supernatural heaven. Eccles calls Rabbit a mystic. Rabbit's "mysticism" is closely linked to his experience of sexuality. Across the road from Ruth's room is a church window "seeming to make a hole where he looked through into underlying brightness." Updike's story "Wife Wooing" in *Pigeon Feathers* mentions the psychologists' theory that rose windows in churches are vaginal symbols, and the husband in this story recalls the rose-window patterns made on the ceiling by a kerosene heater when he was on his honeymoon. Rabbit can conceive of a high and holy joy. But religion remains outside the room he is in, and at the end of the book the light has been extinguished in the church and the bright window is dark. He does not understand that the motions of grace are effective only when we acknowledge our solidarity with others and repent for our selfish hardness of heart.

Eccles is seen once by Rabbit standing behind a car, so that his head seems on a platter. He is a John the Baptist calling to repentance. He chides Rabbit for returning to his home to collect clean shirts, while trampling upon other decencies. But he does not only scold; he shows how forgiveness may be found. He takes Rabbit on the golf course. On the greens, which resemble pagan groves, Rabbit finds himself naming the irons Janice and the woods—the natural, sympathetic material— Ruth. But his imagination is not wholly sexual, since the hole he aims for becomes his home, with his grandfather upstairs in the sky above. And Eccles, "his grubby shirt like a white flag of forgiveness," is guiding him home. Eccles' lesson follows the lines of Updike's story "Intercession," in *The Same Door.* There, a guilt-ridden man plays golf with an imaginative boy and is infuriated because the boy will not play by the rules and refuses to count wasted shots. Rabbit too is angered by Eccles making him try over again when he fails. What he objects to is the assumption that his strokes are past counting. Eccles, of course, knows that Grace comes only when we cease to try to live by Law; forgiveness follows the realization that our sins are too many for us to atone for them ourselves.

At least, something in Eccles knows this. Throughout *Rabbit, Run* the motions of grace are present, yet the instruments mediating grace are woefully inadequate. Young Jack Eccles is the third of an ecclesiastical series. His grandfather was a near-Unitarian and his father rigidly High Church; both were equally successful and popular. His predecessor in his present parish was another much admired cleric. So he lives under a churchly shadow, haunted by the thought that he follows his calling to please an earthly rather than a heavenly father, and conscious that he is being judged constantly to be inadequate for his position. His insecurity is increased by his wife Lucy, a Freudian who loses no opportunity to remind him that she thinks Christianity a neurotic religion involving him daily in a childish retreat from reality. And he draws criticism also from beyond his own home and congregation. When he visits the elderly Lutheran minister of the Angstrom family, Fritz Kruppenbach, the latter comes in from mowing the lawn. Standing in his sweaty undershirt he proceeds to tell Eccles that his job is not to run around trying to make everything smooth but to be an exemplar of faith, so that he can offer Christ to the people. Incensed, yet at the same time feeling guilty, Eccles escapes from the old man who has urged him to be hot for Christ. He cools himself with a vanilla soda in the local drugstore.

Dressed in his undershirt as though in vestments, Kruppenbach gives Eccles the stripped-down essentials of the faith that alone can make his ministry effective. Nevertheless, the young clergyman continues to believe—as everyone else, including Kruppenbach, does not—that Rabbit is worth saving. Rabbit is drawn to him and to the way of life for which the Church stands, although he realizes that his own vague faith in Something out there that is trying to find him is actually as definite as anything Eccles has to offer him. "Soggy" is his summing up of how Eccles strikes him.

Thus Rabbit is thrown back upon his previous trust in his own intuitions. He loses hope after discovering how the coming of baby June has failed to bring warmth into the home. Janice (i.e., January-ice) is as cold as ever. She is the blue-veined ice that he once dreamed to be in his mother's ice-box. Before Rabbit's last run into blankness, he tries to get in touch with Eccles. But communication finally breaks down between them. Lucy Eccles, furious after the time Rabbit let her know he thought she had unconsciously propositioned him, hangs up when he telephones the rectory. So *Rabbit, Run* ends with man's hard heart still rejecting grace. There is little forgiveness amongst nominal Christians, while in the official *ecclesia* forgiveness is no longer proclaimed with conviction. As Rabbit runs the round church window, that should be bright, is a dark circle "because of church poverty or the late summer nights or just carelessness."

That not all human hearts are hardened against the motions of grace is evident in *The Centaur* (1963), a book originally planned to be a contrasting companion to *Rabbit, Run*. The

novel portrays a man as socially responsible as Rabbit Angstrom is irresponsible. George Caldwell, an Olinger high-school
teacher, is seen through the eyes of his adolescent child Peter, in
the setting of Updike's own home. This character, already
sketched in some detail as David's father George of "Pigeon
Feathers," is drawn with great affection. Updike has adopted an
ambitious plan whereby George is viewed in alternating scenes
as a man and as Chiron, the wise centaur and teacher of the
children of Olympus, who, wounded by an arrow, surrenders his
immortality in exchange for the pardon of Prometheus.

The Centaur won the National Book Award for the year. It
is doubtful, though, whether the device of yoking an explicit
mythology to a naturalistic narrative is artistically justified, in
spite of the near-precedent in Joyce's *Ulysses*. At any rate,
Updike has not used it since. There is certainly much ingenuity
expended in matching the two levels whereby, when Olinger
becomes Olympus, the high-school principal Zimmerman dou-
bles as Zeus, the garage-man Hummel as Hephaestus the smith
of the gods, and so on. But Peter is an inadequate Prometheus,
for his status in Olinger is too lowly to make his impiety
significant. And George Caldwell's sacrificial life stands in its
own right, gaining little from being assimilated to the specific
sacrifice of Chiron. Besides, Greek myth is so unfamiliar today
that even the addition of an index—added, Updike tells us, at
his wife's suggestion—hardly helps us to move with comfort
between the mortals and the immortals.

Once again, it is the book's motto that announces its intention. This time, Karl Barth is the source:

> Heaven is the creation inconceivable to man, earth the creation
> conceivable to him. He himself is the creature on the boundary
> between heaven and earth.

The story begins with Caldwell, a lax disciplinarian, having a
metal arrow shot into his ankle by a student. After Hummel has
removed it, Caldwell returns to the next class and tells the story
of the evolution of the world, with Zimmerman in the classroom
sitting in judgment upon his performance. He describes the
beginning of the universe in the dispersal of radiant energy, the
introduction of certain death as opposed to random extinction
by the coming of co-operative life with the volvox, and lastly—
just as the buzzer goes—the appearance of "a tragic animal"
called Man. The class is inattentive, and Zimmerman exudes a

lechery that smells. In anger, Caldwell strikes an unpleasant boy who is pawing a girl, "a smutty little tramp from outside Olinger."

This is earth, the conceivable sphere. Its glories culminate in the tragic bestiality of a humanity that has the stench of Swift's *yahoos.*

The last pages of *The Centaur* show Chiron surrendering himself to death, and setting forth the lesson learned by the children of Olympus. First, Zeus is to be worshipped. Second, the five rivers of the dead are listed. Third, the fifty daughters of Nereus, each protecting one region of the inhabited earth, are named. Fourth, a hero is defined as a king sacrificed to Hera.

This is the wisdom of heaven, the inconceivable. In heaven's perspective the divine order rules over the whole world, ordains death, and opens to man a heroic role through the service of Hera, the patroness of sacred marriage.

Man is on the boundary between heaven and earth. Caldwell fears that Zimmerman will dismiss him because he has stumbled upon some of the principal's shady dealings, and Zimmerman knows that Peter has found out about them too. But Zimmerman simply commends him as a good teacher, and writes in his report that Caldwell should learn to draw out the human values inherent in science. Peter's father has indeed learned how to see earth in the perspective of heaven. And he is a hero, the apparently amiable but ineffective family man who can face death as the condition of purposeful existence, knowing that each generation must pass away so that the next may follow and grow in wisdom.

All this is neat, but a little too contrived. The really effective passages in the novel are quite apart from the classical myth, or break away from the pagan story into the Christian. Caldwell is the first of six generations of his family not to be a minister. His father died having lost his faith. Caldwell knows that knowledge by itself is destructive of faith, and teaches Peter that vision matters more than facts. Peter becomes a painter. Yet he feels that his choice is to some degree a decline in greatness, a step down to a lower level of awareness. Then, Updike describes a great snowstorm covering the district and stopping all the business of men. The storm is described in terms of the diffusion of energy characterizing the scientific picture of the beginning of the physical universe. It is also seen as a complex overlay of patterned beauty, snow upon snow, covering the earth from heaven, and recreating Bethlehem. The snow comes out of a violet and yellow sky—the identical sky of *The Poorhouse Fair* that seemed so troubled. And Peter's father emerges from the storm feeling refreshed as never before.

In addition, the basketball game theme of *Rabbit, Run* features in *The Centaur*. Vera Hummel, *alias* Aphrodite the goddess of sexual love, is there talking to a minister whose faith is like "dead metal." To Caldwell the auditorium smells of lust and death. On this same evening Peter declares his love to Penny Fogelman. Much more than lust is here, for Penny does not recoil from Peter's psoriasis which is the shadow on his life. "I knew you had a skin thing," she says, and her love is outgoing affection, sealed with compassion. This, too, is the night when Zimmerman calls Peter's father a good teacher, quoting first St. Paul's words about speaking the truth in love. Heaven shines through earth's dark.

Ultimately, the wisdom of Chiron is not rooted in Olympus. He remembers how, as young George, he had been nauseated by the blasphemous and cruel laughter coming through the double doors of a saloon. His father, walking beside him in his clerical collar, had smiled and said, "All joy belongs to the Lord." Even in the tragic confusions of the world the good patterns created by God persist. "Only goodness lives. But it does live." The science teacher knows in the pattern of his own life the pattern prefigured in the volvox. In the surrender of one's life for others there is perfect freedom. Yet the possibility of such freedom comes only after God has visited the earth, giving grace upon grace, in Bethlehem. The true inspiration of *The Centaur* is not pagan myth but Christian history.

V

HARMONY AND DISCORD

THE MUSIC SCHOOL AND *OF THE FARM*

In *The Centaur* George Caldwell goes into a lavatory during the basketball match at Olinger High. He sees there, gouged into the wall, a four-letter word of which three letters have been altered to make the word spell BOOK. He wonders whether his son has done this.

Peter Caldwell grows up to be a painter. Art, one of Updike's three "mysteries," can work just such a transformation as Peter's father observed. It can change man's animality into civilized reflection upon truth. Peter's vocation as an artist is barely touched on in *The Centaur*, so that we might well imagine that the next stage in Updike's work would be to explore the transition from sexuality to art in the same way that he has already explored the transition from sexuality to religion.

Nevertheless, this does not happen. Updike's story "The Archangel" in *Pigeon Feathers* shows how seriously he takes the artistic vision, yet he seems to believe that art should always turn outward to life rather than narcissistically contemplate itself. For him art is a craft fit for working men, and not an aesthetic exercise for idlers. Thus his latest fiction moves further into the problem of how the contemporary world is to find its necessary relation to the total pattern on the universe.

In his third collection of short stories, *The Music School* (1966), and his fourth novel, *Of the Farm* (1966), he begins again with sexuality in order to probe the possibility for our living daily in a state of natural piety and for our pressing through to a vision of heavenly grace. The sexuality he concentrates upon, though, is no longer that of the awakening adolescent or of the young married man meeting his first disillusioning shock when his dreams are shipwrecked on the rocks of actuality. Nor is it that of the mature "hero," ready to sacrifice himself for the sacred joy of marriage. Updike now asks his contemporaries, parents of growing children, where they think they are going and whether they have resources for going anywhere. In sexual terms he asks whether they serve Aphrodite or Hera. In religious terms, he asks whether they have found a God to whom they can pray, and rise forgiven.

In portraying the passage from youth to the frontiers of middle age, Updike's prose has shed much of its ebullient brilliance. The "middleness" which he has always wished to describe seems to have settled itself into muted tones and sad colors. He foreshadowed the change already in *Pigeon Feathers,* in a story ("Dear Alexandros") which marks his first attempt to deal with husbands and wives separating:

> It is autumn now in New York City. The sad little trees along the somewhat sad little street where I live now are turning yellow, the ones that are not already dead.

It is hardly surprising that many of the critics should complain that the writer is writing himself out, and that he has really nothing to say. It is true that there is little action in his recent fiction, little drama of the clash of wills releasing showers of sparks, and hardly anything of his previous rapturous celebration of the flesh or high-spirited castigation of sophisticated folly. Yet, if this writing is at the opposite extreme of, say, the violent turmoil of Albee's *Who's Afraid of Virginia Woolf?* it is because Updike does not think of human beings as empty vessels that can be counted on to make any amount of noise. He thinks of them as musical instruments which, even though untuned, can reverberate with the sounds of eternity.

The opening sentence of the short story "The Music School" seems to question that last statement, for it runs: "My name is Alfred Schweigen and I exist in time." *Schweigen,* to keep silent: Alfred does not make music and no longer hopes for eternal life. But, when taking his daughter for her music class in the basement of "a huge Baptist church," he is among golden plates (for the collection) and angelic children and sounds that "arrive like hints of another world." He thinks how hard it is to learn the language of music, to translate notes on paper into actual harmonies, in a progress from vision to *vision.* His daughter is happily contented after her lesson, which is to her "like a meal." As for him, he is here only because his wife is at the psychiatrist's—the consequence of his being unfaithful to her.

41

"My friends are like me. We are all pilgrims, faltering toward divorce."

Updike sets the stage neatly. Alfred Schweigen is making excuses for himself. He could play if he had the will, for he has access to the world beyond time. He is a writer. He knows the difference between ordinary sight and spiritual vision; and the huge Baptist church above him is the world in which repentance and rebirth are offered. He is within the sphere of grace, if no more than in its lower levels. What prevents him from the assured vision of harmony achieved is his unfaithfulness to his wife, a sin driving her out to seek an interim peace without hope of the true reconciliation that heaven alone can give. He also goes to a psychiatrist, but his still unbroken link with his daughter brings him to this better hope. He sees the girl come refreshed from her lesson, and comments, "I die (I think I am dying) at her feet."

Updike, however, does not leave the matter there. He clinches the argument with Alfred's reflections upon two recent experiences. One is a conversation with a young priest, who explains that new developments in theology have led to the making of sacramental wafers solid enough to be chewed rather than dissolve in the mouth. The other is the news of a scientist being shot while at the dining-room table with his wife and five children. Alfred has been planning to write a novel around a computer programmer involved with two women, and the murder sets him thinking about the "new men" of science who seem to live beyond the guilt and strain of being a thinking animal. The idea stirs a memory. The memory is of sharing in the communion service in a country church, where confession led to rising refreshed.

"The host is the world," he concludes. This means that the faith once giving heart to a simpler society must be palpably experienced in our more complex one. For there are actually no "new men" around. The lust producing adultery and the hatred producing murder are unchanged elements of all human experience. The immaterial world and the material one, so Alfred guesses, interact whether or not we believe in the unseen. What Alfred lacks is the will to chew the host, to die to sin really and not just in thought, for the sake of his daughter. Unless his repentance at the Lord's Table can be as brutally effective as the impact of the bullet that killed the scientist at his family table,

Alfred will have gone to the music school and yet still live, untaught, without harmony.

Most of the other stories in *The Music School* take up aspects of the theme which this story lays out so fully. A couple are coldly satiric about a society trusting in psychiatrists and lawyers to regulate love. "Four Sides of One Story" strips the Tristram and Iseult legend of glamor by putting it into modern dress. "My Lover has Dirty Fingernails" scratches the glossy, exquisitely finished surface of a psychiatrist's office, with its matching occupants, and reveals underlying filth. We are not in earnest today when we write BOOK over the obscene word, Updike seems to suggest. Lavatories still mean more to us than libraries, sensuality than science. Two more stories, "The Stare" and "The Morning," present different versions of one situation: a man refuses to marry his mistress, and realizes too late that the hurt he has given is beyond repair.

Of the Farm is a deceptive book—so transparent-looking, so complex in pattern. The material shown in *The Music School* is combined with the lesson of *The Poorhouse Fair*. Joey Robinson, deciding to marry his mistress instead of sending her away, has made the full pilgrimage to divorce. With his new wife Peggy (also divorced) and her son Richard he spends three days visiting his mother at the family farm in Pennsylvania. Mrs. Robinson greets them with the cry, "Pilgrims!"

Peggy resembles physically the Aphrodite of *The Centaur*. In her vulgar sensuality she embodies the negative side of sexuality that Updike stresses continually in his recent writings. She is a walking example of the regression from BOOK to the obscene, for her first husband, McCabe, is an assistant dean at Yale, and Joey sees the place in which his second marriage was solemnized as a lavatory. Thus literacy gives way to sensuality. Peggy is called stupid by Joey's mother, and Joey has to agree. She certainly is not well read, being conspicuously uninformed about the Bible; her natural bent is for four-letter words, which become the normal idiom of conversation between her and her husband. Yet, while Joey married Peggy for her body, his first wife Joan attracted him initially because she reminded him of Wordsworth's Lucy and "The Solitary Reaper." Joey's courtship began with BOOK. It has declined catastrophically into the lavatory.

The regressive path that led Joey to his divorce and remarriage is described by Joey himself in a bedtime story he tells to Richard. Joey says that a frog went down inside himself to look for a treasure there, but became smaller and smaller and never found the treasure. When the boy asks whether the frog died, Joey says that he was just hibernating; later, he climbed up inside himself, pulled up the shades of his eyelids, and looked out again at the blue sky. The question that emerges is whether Joey, the frog that has shrunk to nothingness through his search for the treasure that he imagines to be found in sexuality, will open his eyes to the world of creative, natural life represented by the farm.

The frog climbed down inside himself when the leaves were falling, in the autumn of faithlessness. Again, as in "Dear Alexandros," the season of the decay of love is marked as the season of *yellow* leaves. When the frog awoke, he saw blue sky. Joey recalls that, when he first met Peggy, she was wearing a yellow dress and Joan a blue one. He is troubled by a portrait photograph of Joan, taken shortly after their marriage, on the farmhouse wall. He is fighting against his memories, not wishing to see again the blue of Joan's dress, or the blue heaven that had been their love. Above all, he does not wish to revive the imaginative vision of his youth which intuitively connected Joan with those poems of Wordsworth dealing with solitude, pain, and loss. His mother wanted him to be a poet. He keeps the shades pulled down upon the poetry of existence.

Joey's mother is a familiar figure in the world of Updike's fiction. Mary Robinson resembles David's mother Elsie in "Pigeon Feathers" and Peter's mother Cassie (Ceres) in *The Centaur*. Her late husband's name, like the husbands of Elsie and Cassie, is George. And the history of the family's various moves, from the farm to Olinger and back again, reproduces the history of Updike's parents and grandparents. But, renamed Mary, this mother is also the virgin land of American history and the sorrowing mother left alone to mourn.

Mary Robinson has not been able to use the land for farming. Richard, his father's son in his intellectual curiosity, wants to know what is the use of a farm that nobody farms. Mrs. Robinson says that the land, like people, gets very tired and needs rest. She proposes that the two of them should keep a "people sanctuary," and Richard becomes interested in the ways of nature. But the boy, who is partly Joey made young again (Joey calls him "frog"), is too much a product of the restless city civilization to be won over entirely. Peggy is intensely jealous of the older woman's success in gaining his affection, and asserts her power by forbidding Richard to drive the farm tractor.

Mrs. Robinson recognizes that she is too old and weak to bring either her son or his step-son into the people-sanctuary. Neither will open his eyes to the sanctified life of the farm. The weather in this novel significantly reverses the weather pattern of *The Poorhouse Fair*. The second day at the farm begins with clear blue skies and intense heat—the spiritual color of blue, but marked also by the blankness of sensuality (as in *Rabbit, Run*) as well as by its intense warmth, a warmth too frantic to last. It culminates in a rainstorm, forcing Joey to stop mowing the weeds in the field, which is an occupation he identifies with the sexual act. The weeds, which Joey's mother knows must be cut regularly, will grow again after the rain. So Mrs. Robinson is convinced that the task of looking after the farm is beyond her, and her son will not stay to do it for her. Richard, forbidden to learn the craft of husbandry, cannot attempt it. And thus there is no one left to work either on the land or at the craft of being a good husband and responsible father of children.

At the end of the novel, accepting her approaching death and her loss of family, she asks Joey not to sell her farm cheap. "*Your* farm?" her son replies. "I've always thought of it as our farm."

Of the Farm is a tragic story. It is not merely that Mary Robinson, who is "of the farm" and of the rich, natural life that it represents, is left alone to die, deprived of grandchildren who might inherit the land she loves. The tragedy is Joey's, who has by his own decision lost his past and given away his children. He recognizes that he cannot "see" both Peggy and the farm at once, so he gives up the farm. Change and death are inevitable on a farm; but there is continuity there, and mutual support between the generations. Joey has lost the right to say "our" of anything. He cannot say to Peggy that Richard is "our" child. He cannot share a common past with her—he does not even know the circumstances that led to Peggy's divorce. Significantly, Peggy has never referred to McCabe by his first name. The links that tie us to nature and to one another have all been broken, and the faith that alone supports human values has been made impossible. Joey, the frog who seeks a treasure, has, all unknowingly, sold it cheap.

With Updike, Wordsworth is never far away.

> The world is too much with us; late and soon,
> Getting and spending, we lay waste our powers:
> Little we see in nature that is ours;
> We have given our heart away, a sordid boon!
>
> For this, for everything, we are out of tune;
> It moves us not.—Great God! I'd rather be
> A pagan suckled in a creed outworn;
> So might I, standing on this pleasant lea,
> Have glimpses that would make me less forlorn. . . .

In *The Centaur* Updike takes Wordsworth literally, reviving the pagan Olympians to give heart to the present, although he knows Christianity alone can bring true healing power. In *The Music School* he traces the pilgrim way of the modern age as it progresses from discord to complete loss of the music of the universe. And in *Of the Farm* he stands upon a "pleasant lea" and sees a forlorn generation speeding off in cars into nothingness, the enduring links with nature undiscerned. Joey has filled his mother's house with expensive, unsuitable presents, usually sent late. But he never has found the pearl of great price. Natural piety was destroyed when he disobeyed, as his mother reminds him, the biblical command "Cleave to thy wife." Mary Robinson is not surprised, though she is angered, at his choosing a stupid woman to take the place of an imaginative one. Her explanation is simple and direct. "See, you forgot God."

SELECTED BIBLIOGRAPHY

I. WORKS BY JOHN UPDIKE

Except for *The Carpentered Hen,* published by Harper and Brothers, New York, all of Updike's books have been published in the first instance by Alfred A. Knopf, New York.

NOVELS

The Poorhouse Fair	1959
Rabbit, Run	1960
The Centaur	1963
Of the Farm	1965

COLLECTIONS OF SHORT STORIES

The Same Door	1959
Pigeon Feathers and Other Stories	1962
The Music School	1966
also:	
Olinger Stories: A Selection (Vintage Books)	1964

COLLECTIONS OF POEMS

The Carpentered Hen and Other Tame Creatures	1958
Telephone Poles and Other Poems	1963

ESSAYS

Assorted Prose	1965

FOR CHILDREN

The Magic Flute, By Wolfgang Amadeus Mozart	1962
	(With Warren Chappell)
The Ring, By Richard Wagner (With Warren Chappell)	1964
A Child's Calendar	1965

UNCOLLECTED SHORT STORIES

"The Witnesses," *New Yorker,* August 13, 1966.
"The Pro," *New Yorker,* September 17, 1966.
"Bech in Rumania," *New Yorker,* October 8, 1966.
"Your Lover Just Called," *Harper's Magazine,* January 1967.
"The Taste of Metal," *New Yorker,* March 11, 1967.

II. SOME CRITICAL ESSAYS, ETC., ON UPDIKE

Aldridge, John W. "The Private Vice of John Updike," *Time to Murder and Create; The Contemporary Novel in Crisis* (New York: David McKay, 1966).

Brenner, Gerry. "Rabbit Run: John Updike's Criticism of the 'Return to Nature,'" *Twentieth Century Literature,* 12 (April, 1966).

Detweiler, Robert. "John Updike and the Indictment of Culture-Protestantism," *Four Spiritual Crises in Mid-Century American Fiction* (Gainesville: University of Florida Press, 1964).

Doner, Dean. "Rabbit Angstrom's Unseen World" in *New World Writing,* 20 (1962).

Duncan, Graham H. "The Thing Itself in *Rabbit, Run,"* *English Record,* 13 (April, 1963).

Finklestein, Sidney. "Acceptance of Alienation: John Updike and James Purdy," *Existentialism and Alienation in American Literature* (New York: International Publishers, 1965).

Galloway, David D. "The Absurd Man as Saint: The Novels of John Updike," *The Absurd Hero in American Fiction, Updike, Styron, Bellow and Salinger* (Austin: University of Texas, 1966).

Hicks, Granville. "Generations of the Fifties: Malamud, Gold, and Updike," *The Creative Present,* ed. Norma Balakian and Charles Simmons (New York: Doubleday, 1963).

—————. "Mysteries of the Commonplace," *The Saturday Review of Literature,* 45 (March 17, 1962).

Howard, Jane. "Can a Nice Novelist Finish First?" *Life* (November 4, 1966).

Lacourse, Guerin. "The Innocence of John Updike," *Commonweal,* 78 (May 10, 1963).

Mizener, Arthur. "The American Hero as High-School Boy," *The Sense of Life in the Modern Novel* (New York: Houghton Mifflin, **1964).**

Murphy, Richard W. "John Updike," *Horizon,* 4 (March, 1962).

Novak, Michael. "Updike's Quest for Liturgy," *Commonweal,* 78 (May 10, 1963).

O'Connor, William Van. "John Updike and William Styron: The Burden of Talent," *Contemporary American Novelists,* ed. Harry T. Moore (Carbondale: Southern Illinois University Press, 1964).

Podhoretz, Norman. "A Dissent on Updike," *Doings and Undoings; the Fifties and After in American Writing* (New York: Noonday Press, 1964).

Tate, Sister Judith M. "John Updike: Of Rabbits and Centaurs," *Critic,* 22 (February-March, 1964).

Ward, J. A. "John Updike's Fiction," *Critique,* 5 (Spring-Summer, 1962).

22   20 2